IT'S YOUR BID

TONY SOWTER

Foreword by BOBBY WOLFF

HOW TO PLAY BRIDGE

NTC Publishing Group

NTC/Contemporary Publishing Company

Library of Congress Cataloging-in-Publication Data is on file at the United States Library of Congress

Published by NTC Publishing Group
An imprint of NTC/Contemporary Publishing Company
Copyright © 1998 by Tony Sowter
4255 West Touhy Avenue, Lincolnwood (Chicago), Illinois 60646-1975 U.S.A.
Printed in Singapore
International Standard Book Number:
0-8442-2564-9

contents

foreword

Bridge is a game enjoyed by many millions of players all over the world.

In these days of rising commercial pressures, increasing leisure and greater longevity, bridge has the potential to break down social and ethnic barriers and to keep the wheels of the brain turning in both the old and the young. Apart from that, bridge at whatever level is a very inexpensive game; all you need to play is a flat surface that the four players can sit round with a pack of cards and, of course, an understanding of how to play the game.

It is for these reasons that I am particularly pleased to welcome the 'How to Play Bridge' series which has been specially designed to make the game easy to follow for beginners, no matter what their age. I believe that you will find the whole series well presented and particularly easy to read.

It is a curious fact, that over the years many of the great bridge authors have been British. Names like Victor Mollo, Hugh Kelsey, Skid Simon and Terence Reese still figure prominently in the USA lists of the greatest selling bridge books, so the fact that this series of books has been generated in Great Britain comes as no real surprise. I happen to know that all the authors have played bridge at International level so, in general terms, they should know what they are talking about. Furthermore, all of the books are based on the methods that are played all over the United States today. So, once you have learnt, you should have little difficulty in getting a game whenever you want to.

I believe that after studying the 'How to Play Bridge' series you will not only be off to a good start, you will be totally enthralled by this great game.

Bobby Wolff
Dallas, Texas
March 1997

before we begin

basic hand evaluation

Most modern bidding systems are built around the idea of points, which are a rough measure of the strength of a hand. For our purposes, there are three basic types of points that we are interested in.

High Card Points (HCP) are measured on the simple scale:

An Ace	=	4
A King	=	3
A Queen	=	2
A Jack	=	1

So, quite clearly, there are 10 available HCP in every suit and, as there are four suits in the pack, there are a total of 40 HCP in the pack. So, an average hand will include exactly 10 HCP.

High Card Points (HCP)
An Ace	=	4
A King	=	3
A Queen	=	2
A Jack	=	1

Distributional Points are designed to value the extra playing strength of a long suit. As a simple guideline, add one point for each card in excess of four in any suit.

Support Points are designed to value the extra playing strength if you find a good fit with your partner.

When you know you have an eight-card fit, add:

1 points for a doubleton
2 points for a singleton
3 points for a void

With a nine card fit add:

2 points for a doubleton
3 points for a singleton
4 points for a void.

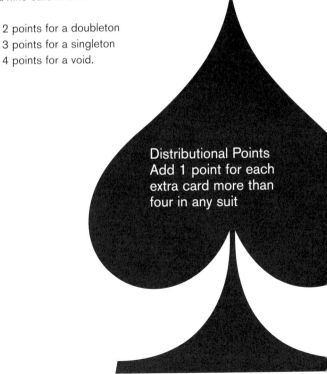

Distributional Points
Add 1 point for each
extra card more than
four in any suit

targets

There are 40 High Card Points in the pack, so if these were the only determinant of trick-taking potential, each three points would be worth a trick.

As 9 tricks is the target to make 3NT, you might expect 27 points to be the target for your combined assets to make the game – however, as even with the flattest distribution, you hope to make something out of your long cards, 26 points should be enough on average.

Similarly, to make 10 tricks in four of a major, you might expect to need 30 points. However, with an eight-card trump fit unless you both have matching distributions you would normally expect to make at least one extra trick by ruffing. This reduces the target to 27, and, just as before, the opportunity to make an extra trick from length reduces the target to 26.

With 26 points between the 2 hands, aim to play in game. Either 3NT or 4♥/♠ if you have an 8 card fit

Making game in a minor takes 11 tricks, so with an eight-card fit you need 29 points, three more points than for four of a major. In the same way, the target for a small slam (12 tricks) with an eight-card fit should be 32 points, subject, of course, to you not having two immediate losers. In no trumps, increase the point count required to 33 or 34.

what is bidding all about?

The whole point of bidding is to conduct a useful discussion with your partner in order to determine a suitable contract for your side to play in. In reality, there are so many possible combinations of hands that it is totally impossible to bid with 100% accuracy especially at a low level. However, by adopting a sensible set of rules as to the meaning of the bids you make, it is possible to build an increasingly accurate picture of your hand.

Before starting to look at the set of rules which are going to govern your bidding, let's look at a few bidding sequences to see what we are trying to achieve.

1.	West	East
	1 ♠ (i)	2 ♥ (ii)
	2NT (iii)	3 ♦ (iv)
	3 ♥ (v)	4 ♥ (vi)
	Pass	

So, what is going on?

(i) When West opens the bidding 1♠ he tells his partner that he holds at least 13 points and at least five spades.

(ii) East's response shows enough strength to bid at the two level, at least 10 points say, with at least five hearts.

(iii) West's second bid, technically described as his rebid, describes his hand further. By rebidding no trumps at minimum level he is showing a minimum strength opening bid in the 13-15 point range. Furthermore, East should now know that his partner has a balanced hand, probably 5-2-3-3 distribution down the suits without particularly good spades (he might have rebid 2♠ not 2NT) and without particularly good hearts (he might have supported hearts if he knew that the partnership had 8 hearts between them).

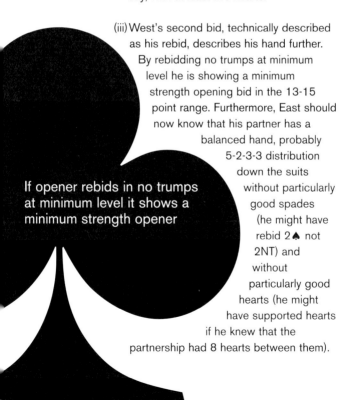

If opener rebids in no trumps at minimum level it shows a minimum strength opener

(iv) When East bids on he clearly must have more than a minimum to have bid at the two level for he could have passed West's 2NT bid and he is showing a second suit. West should expect East to have at least five hearts and at least four diamonds.

Build up a picture of your hand

(v) West's 3♥ bid is interesting. With three cards in hearts he should have supported hearts on the previous round, so this 3♥ bid is consistent with West holding a good doubleton. At the same time, if West had a very good holding in clubs, surely he would have suggested that 3NT should be the final contract not 4♥, so East should really know that West's clubs are not that good.

(vi) On the basis of all this information, East decides that the best contract for his side will be 4♥.

In effect, West opened the bidding and over the course of three rounds of bidding gave a fairly accurate picture of his hand, which is something like:

♠ AK965
♥ K5
♦ K85
♣ 1072

13 HCP plus one distributional point making a total of 14, enough to open the bidding but only a minimum opener. Five spades shown by the opening bid, a balanced hand without support for his partner's hearts shown by the 2NT rebid and poor clubs with secondary heart support shown by the bid of 3♥.

Opening 1♥ or 1♠ shows 5 cards in the suit

East showed a good hand with hearts and diamonds but then chose the contract when West owned up to a modicum of heart support. East's hand could easily be:

♠ 7
♥ AQJ106
♦ AQ72
♣ 943

Looking at the combined hands, 3NT is not a bad contract failing only when the defence can take five tricks in clubs but it would take another Hiroshima to beat 4♥.

2.

West	East
1 ♦ (i)	1 ♠ (ii)
1NT(iii)	2NT(iv)
3NT(v)	Pass

(i) West's opening shows 13+ points and at least four diamonds. West might have a second suit but it will not be longer than his diamond suit.

(ii) East must have at least 6 points to keep the bidding open and he has at least four spades. If he only has four spades then he won't have four hearts because he would have responded in his lower four card suit.

(iii) Once again West has a minimum opener and a balanced hand, his rebid limiting his hand to a range of 13-15 points and he does not have primary support for spades otherwise he would have rebid 2♠.

(iv) East knows that his partner has somewhere between 13 and 15 points and he knows that his side will need about 26 points to make 3NT, nine tricks in no trumps is enough for game. There would be no point in him raising the level of the contract to 2NT if he knew that there was no possibility of making game and he would raise directly to 3NT if he knew that his side had enough points to try and make game. Therefore, 2NT is an invitational bid, inviting the opener to press on to game with a maximum hand for his 1NT rebid or pass otherwise.

(v) West looks at his hand and decides that he holds a maximum rather than a minimum. Accordingly, he bids on to 3NT as requested.

Once again, West built up a picture of his hand over three rounds which might be something like:

♠ J6
♥ KJ86
♦ AQJ5
♣ QJ6

First he showed at least 13 points, normally with four diamonds and no other longer suit. Then his 1NT rebid clarified that he actually had a balanced hand in the 13-15 point range without primary spade support. Then he showed that he was maximum for his 1NT bid by bidding on to 3NT when his partner issued an invitation.

Meanwhile, East showed at least four spades but not more than five as he would have made more effort to play in spades, and a hand strong enough to invite his partner to bid game but not strong enough to bid game himself. East might hold something like:

♠ Q1074
♥ AQ5
♦ K6
♣ 10842

When West rebid 1NT, East knew that his side held somewhere in the range of 24 to 26 points so that if his partner was maximum there should be fair play to make nine tricks.

On the combined hands, West should have no difficulty making nine tricks. With eight tricks waiting in the red suits, all he has to do is establish one trick in either black suit. Meanwhile, the best the defence can do will be to cash the ace and king in both black suits.

An opening bid of 1♦ shows 13+ points and normally at least 4 diamonds

3.   West   East
            1NT(i)   2♠(ii)

(i)   1NT is by far the most descriptive opening bid at the one-level. It shows a balanced hand within a very limited range of points. In our system, the 1NT shows any 4-4-3-2, 4-3-3-3 or 5-3-3-2 hand within the range of 16-18 points.

(ii) Because West has been able to describe his hand so accurately with just one bid, East is able to choose the contract. In this case, he elects to play in 2♠ having a weak hand with a long spade suit.

The two hands might well be:

	♠ K104				♠ J98532
	♥ AK52				♥ 76
	♦ KQ6				♦ 732
	♣ Q65				♣ 82

As you can see, West has a 3-4-3-3 distribution with 17 points and, while East only has 1 HCP, two spades is an excellent contract which will succeed most of the time. This is a good illustration of the advantage of playing with the weak hand's long suit as trumps.

4.

West	*East*
1NT(i)	3♠(ii)
4♠(iii)	Pass

(i) Once again, West has opened with this most descriptive of bids to show a balanced hand in the 16-18 point range.

(ii) However, this time East has enough values for game, his jump to 3♠ shows a five card suit and asks West to bid either 3NT or 4♠.

(iii) On this particular hand, having three spades in his own hand, West chooses to play in the major suit game. However, if he had had only two spades he would have bid 3NT.

The full hands might be:

♠ K104		**N**	♠ AQ985
♥ AK52	**W**	**E**	♥ 76
♦ KQ6		**S**	♦ A432
♣ Q65			♣ 82

Notice that despite the fact that the West hand is totally flat, 4♠ is a much better contract than 3NT. It will take bad breaks in both spades and diamonds to threaten 4♠ while the defence might easily take the first five club tricks against a contract of 3NT.

An opening bid of 1NT shows a balanced hand of 16-18 points

5.	West	East
	1♠(i)	1NT(ii)
	2♥(iii)	3♥(iv)
	Pass(v)	

(i) West's opening bid just shows a minimum of 13 points including at least five spades.

(ii) East's response basically shows enough to keep the bidding open, in other words at least six points, not enough to bid at the two level, so less than 10 points and no primary spade support. Very simply, facing a one spade opener, holding a weak hand, responder really only has a choice between supporting his partner to 2♠ or bidding 1NT. Consequently, there is no guarantee that East has a balanced hand at all.

(iii) This time West does not have a balanced hand. His 2♥ rebid shows at least four hearts to go with his five spades and East may pass if he has a weak hand with significantly more hearts than spades. West's strength is slightly better defined than previously inasmuch as if he had about 18 or 19 points he would probably have jumped to 3♥ to make sure that East bids again.

(iv) As it turns out, East has four card heart support and more than a minimum hand, his raise to 3♥ gives West the option of bidding game with some extra values.

(v) West decides that he doesn't really have anything more than he has already promised, so he declines East's invitation.

The full hands might be:

♠ AK642		♠ 87
♥ KQ102	**N**	♥ AJ98
♦ 86	**W E**	♦ QJ52
♣ 75	**S**	♣ 432

With four top losers in the minors and a bit of work
to do in the majors, East/West would have
preferred to stop at a contract of just 2♥.
However, bidding systems are not perfect.

 It was important that East showed his heart
support giving West the chance to decide what
level to play at rather than passing 2♥ only to
find that West had a much better hand and
game was laydown. You only need to add
the ♦K into West's hand for 4♥ to be
the right contract.

**Bidding
systems are
not perfect**

As it is, West should survive in
his contract of 3♥ provided that
the spades break no worse than
4-2 and the hearts divide evenly.

He ruffs the third club, cashed both top
spades, ruffs a spade in dummy, crosses to
his hand with a trump, ruffs another spade with
the ace of trumps and finally crosses back to the
West hand with another trump, to draw the
remaining trump and cash the last spade.
Nine tricks made.

6.

West	East
Pass(i)	1 ♥ (ii)
1 ♠ (ii)	2NT(iii)
3NT(iv)	Pass

(i) This time, West does not have enough points to open the bidding.

(ii) East's opening shows at least 13 points including a five card heart suit.

(iii) West has enough to respond, at least six points, and at least four spades.

(iv) This jump rebid in no trumps also shows a balanced hand and clearly ought to be strong. A 1NT rebid would have shown 13-15 points and if East had between 16 and 18 points, he would have opened 1NT. Therefore, the jump rebid of 2NT shows 19 or 20 points.

(v) West simply raises to 3NT because he can see no advantage in looking for an alternative spot. Therefore, at best, he has very little heart support and he is unlikely to even hold five spades else he might have made more effort to find out if East had any spade support.

The full hands might be:

♠ KJ54	♠ A6
♥ 75	♥ AKQ42
♦ Q75	♦ K102
♣ J1064	♣ K95

Now, at this stage, I have the feeling that you might think that this is all rather too much. However, at least now you know the purpose of this book. It is to introduce you to a bidding system and guiding principles that will help you to describe your hand to your partner and help you to understand what he is trying to tell you about his hand. Learn the principles set down in the following pages and hopefully most of the time, you and your partner should arrive in a sensible contract.

Try to describe
your hand

opening the bidding

As a general rule, if no-one else has bid in front of you, you should open the bidding whenever you hold 13 or more points. This minimum target should include both high card points and distributional points.

Remember, High Card Points (HCP) are measured on the simple scale:

An Ace = 4
A King = 3
A Queen = 2
A Jack = 1

Open the bidding with 13+ points

Distributional Points (DP) are designed to value the extra playing strength of a long suit. As a simple guideline, add one point for each card in excess of four in any suit.

Why then is it right to open the bidding with 13 points. The arithmetic is as follows:

If you have 13 HCP then the other players have 27 between them. So, on average, you would expect your partner to have nine of them. If your partner has nine, then together you have about 22 points which leaves your opponents with only 18. As you expect to have more HCP than your opponents, you should expect to make more tricks than your opponents. You express both this hope and expectation by opening the bidding.

Let's look at some hands:

(a) ♠ AK5   (7 HCP)
     ♥ Q74   (2 HCP)
     ♦ AJ76   (5 HCP)
     ♣ 973   (0 HCP)

Here you have a total of 14 HCP and no distributional points as you don't have a five card suit. However, on high card strength alone you have enough to open the bidding, so bid 1 ♦.

(b) ♠ AK52   (7 HCP)
     ♥ 74   (0 HCP)
     ♦ AJ764   (5 HCP + 1 DP)
     ♣ 97   (0 HCP)

Here you have a total of just 12 HCP but your one Distributional Point takes you to the opening target of 13. Once again, you should open 1 ♦

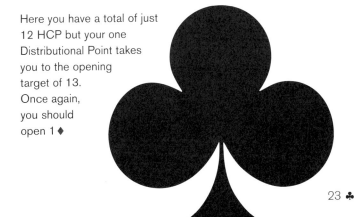

(c) ♠ AJ5   (5 HCP)
     ♥ 74   (0 HCP)
     ♦ AQ7642   (6 HCP + 2 DP)
     ♣ 97   (0 HCP)

This time you have only 11 HCP but your six card diamond suit is worth two additional Distributional Points bringing you up to the target of 13 once again. Open 1♦ again.

(d) ♠ A5   (4 HCP)
     ♥ 4   (2 HCP)
     ♦ AJ764   (5 HCP + 1DP)
     ♣ Q9873   (2 HCP + 1DP)

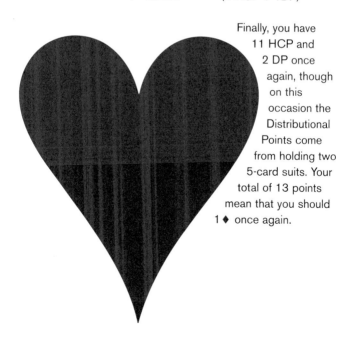

Finally, you have 11 HCP and 2 DP once again, though on this occasion the Distributional Points come from holding two 5-card suits. Your total of 13 points mean that you should 1♦ once again.

balanced hands

Hands of a 4-3-3-3, 4-4-3-2 and 5-3-3-2 distribution are regarded as balanced. These are only three out of a possible 39 distribution types, but they account for nearly half of all possible hands.

A jump rebid in no trumps shows 19-20 points

In most bridge bidding systems an opening bid of 1NT shows a balanced hand within a fairly narrow range of points. We shall adopt a strong no trump opening with the opening bid of 1NT showing between 16 and 18 high card points.

What then are we supposed to do with hands that are either weaker or stronger?

In simple terms, hands that are weaker open with one of a suit and rebid no-trumps at minimum level. This covers minimum opening bids in the point range 13-15.

Hands that are a little stronger, in the 19-20 point range, open with one of a suit and then make a jump rebid in no-trumps. So,

1♣	Pass	1♥	Pass
1NT			

shows 13-15 points, while:

1♣	Pass	1♥	Pass
2NT			

shows 19-20 points.

If partner makes a simple response at the two-level the scheme is unchanged, so

1♦	Pass	2♣	Pass
2NT			

shows a balanced hand in the 13-15 point range, and:

1♦	Pass	2♣	Pass
3NT			

shows a balanced hand with 19-20 points.

An opening bid of 2NT shows an even stronger balanced hand in the range of 21-22 points.

With stronger hands you open with our system's strongest bid, 2♣, then a rebid of 2NT would show 23-24 points and a balanced hand while a jump to 3NT would show 25-26 points.

In all my bridge-playing career, I have only once held a balanced hand with more than 26 points, so it is really not worth the worrying too much about what to bid if you happen to pick up such a hand. Just grin and bear it!

Notice that unless your hand happens to fall into the ranges covered by an opening bid of either 1NT or 2NT, it is going to take two bids to give a general description of your hand. This introduces the important principle that when you are choosing whether to open the bidding and, indeed, what to open, most of the time you need to consider not only your choice of opening bid but also what you plan to bid on the next round. When you have a choice of opening bids, always choose the one that will allow you to describe your hand best on the next round whatever partner responds. Knowing what you plan to do next is known as being prepared.

A 2NT opening shows a balanced hand with 21-22 points

Now, let's look at some examples. How would you plan to describe your hand in each case?

(a) ♠ KJ5   (4 HCP)
     ♥ A1086   (4 HCP)
     ♦ Q105   (2 HCP)
     ♣ AK5   (7 HCP)

As you can see, you have a total of 17 points and a balanced hand, the opening bid of 1NT describes your hand.

(b)   ♠ AJ5   (5 HCP)
       ♥ K53   (3 HCP)
       ♦ Q1076   (2 HCP)
       ♣ QJ5   (3 HCP)

This time, you have a total of 13 HCP, enough to open the bidding but not enough to open 1NT.

So, what is the plan?

Open 1 ♦ and if partner responds with either 1 ♥ or 1 ♠. you can bid 1NT on the next round. If partner responds 2 ♣ you can rebid 2NT.

Notice, that this time it took you two bids to describe your balanced hand. Notice as well that there is no guarantee that you will ever complete the description of your hand.

For example, if partner passes 1 ♦ you might not get the chance to make another bid and if he made a limited response like raising 1 ♦ to 2 ♦ then you would have had no reason to bid again.

(c))   ♠ A86   (4 HCP)
       ♥ AJ752   (5 HCP + 1DP)
       ♦ AK10   (7 HCP)
       ♣ K3   (3 HCP)

This time you have 20 points including one distributional point for the fifth heart. Your plan should be to open 1 ♥, which in our methods shows a five card heart suit, intending to jump in no trumps on the second round.

So if partner responds 1♠, you will describe your hand by jumping to 2NT. However, if partner responds with either 2♣ or 2♦, you will have to jump to 3NT.

(d)   ♠ A86   (4 HCP)
       ♥ A1065   (4 HCP)
       ♦ J75   (1 HCP)
       ♣ A86   (4 HCP)

Once again, with 13 HCP you have to open the bidding but this time you have a different problem. When you opened 1♥ on the last hand it showed a five card heart suit, so what are you supposed to do now that you only have a four card heart suit and no apparent alternative.

Most players in the USA will tell you, that there are tremendous advantages in adopting a system where an opening in either hearts or spades guarantees a five-card suit. However, the downside is that you have to invent some way of dealing with hands like this.

The solution is to open 1♣, planning to rebid 1NT if partner responds either 1♦ or 1♠. If partner bids 1♥ you should support him to 2♥. So, an opening bid of 1♣ only promises three cards in the suit bid.

This deals with all the balanced hands with the noticeable exception of a hand with four cards in both major suits, three diamonds and only two clubs. In this particular case, the solution is to open 1♦.

(e)   ♠ KJ5   (4 HCP)
      ♥ K10864   (3 HCP + 1DP)
      ♦ Q105   (2 HCP)
      ♣ AK   (7 HCP)

This hand poses another conundrum. You have a 5-card heart suit so 1♥ looks like a possible opening but at the same time you have a balanced hand in the 16-18 point range so an opening bid of 1NT beckons. Which bid should take precedence?

Think ahead. When you open the bidding you should also plan a rebid

In my view, the answer should be 1NT which gives a good overall description of the hand despite the fact that you have a five-card major. The problem with a 1♥ opening is that if partner responds in a new suit you have no good rebid. For example, if partner responds 1♠, a 1NT rebid shows 13-15 points while a 2NT rebid shows 19 or 20. You will have absolutely no way of describing your strength accurately.

(f)　　♠ AKJ　　　　(8 HCP)
　　　♥ K10864　　(3 HCP + 1DP)
　　　♦ K105　　　　(3 HCP)
　　　♣ AK　　　　　(7 HCP)

In this final example, you have an even
stronger hand with 22 points including
the one for the fifth heart. Once again,
you should suppress the five card
heart suit and open 2NT.

unbalanced
hands

**An opening bid of 1♣
only promises three
cards in the suit**

If hands with 4-3-3-3,
4-4-3-2 and 5-3-3-2
distribution are described as
balanced, all other distributions can
de described as
unbalanced or distributional
hands.

one-suited hands

Hands with a 6 or 7 card suit and opening
strength are quite easy to handle. Your plan is
simply to open the suit at the one-level and bid the
suit again on the next round at whatever seems to
be the right level. For example:

♠	75	(0 HCP)
♥	AQJ942	(7 HCP + 2 DP)
♦	K5	(3 HCP)
♣	Q105	(2 HCP)

Even counting both distributional points this hand is barely more than a minimum opener. So, open 1♥, planning to rebid 2♥ if partner makes any simple response.

However, improve the hand to:

♠	A5	(4 HCP)
♥	AQJ942	(7 HCP + 2 DP)
♦	A5	(4 HCP)
♣	Q105	(2 HCP)

A jump rebid in the opening suit is invitational

and the hand is far too strong for a simple rebid of 2♥. After all, 4♥ will be a fair contract facing two small hearts and KQx in either pointed suit. How do you give yourself a chance of reaching game when it is sensible without taking an out and out gamble? The answer is to jump to 3♥ on the second round of bidding, asking partner to bid on to game if he has a modicum of suitability for playing in hearts.

two-suited hands

Adherence to the following basic rule will sort out what you should open on most two-suited hands. Whenever you hold two suits always open in the longest suit.

So, for example, consider:

♠	A4	(4 HCP)
♥	KQ1086	(5 HCP + 1 DP)
♦	KJ87	(4 HCP)
♣	87	(0 HCP)

With 14 points and five hearts and four diamonds, you should have no problem. Open 1♥, which shows a five card suit anyway, planning to rebid 2♦ on the second round.

♠	KJ87	(4 HCP)
♥	A4	(4 HCP)
♦	KQ1086	(5 HCP + 1 DP)
♣	87	(0 HCP)

This time life is a bit more complicated. The fact that you should open 1♦ should be clear because that is your longest suit, and if partner responds 1♥ you have an easy rebid of 1♠. Even though the 1♦ opening didn't even guarantee four diamonds when you rebid 1♠ your partner should know that you have an unbalanced hand, and, as

If you open the bidding holding two suits, bid the longer suit first

you would open your longest suit first, he should expect you to have five diamonds and four spades.

Life is more complicated, however, if partner responds 2♣. While it may seem natural to rebid 2♠, most players would think that this should show some extra values, maybe at least 16 points, but all is not lost for you have a comfortable rebid of 2♦.

What should you open with two five card suits? For example, with:

♠	KQ765	(5 HCP + 1 DP)
♥	AJ765	(5 HCP + 1 DP)
♦	K3	(3 HCP)
♣	7	(0 HCP)

With 5 cards in two touching suits, open in the higher suit

With five cards in both majors, should you choose to open 1♥ or 1♠?

Let's look and see what happens if you open 1♥. If partner responds 1NT or two of a minor, then, in order to show his second suit, opener will have to rebid 2♠, thereby pushing the auction to the three-level if partner wants to show preference for hearts.

In contrast, if you open 1♠ and partner responds either 1NT or two of a minor then you can rebid 2♥ and if partner prefers your first suit, he can show this at the two-level by bidding 2♠.

With five cards in two touching suits, it is most economical to open the higher of the two suits. So, with 5-5 in spades and hearts, open 1♠. With 5-5 in hearts and diamonds, open 1♥ and with 5-5 in diamonds and clubs, open 1♦.

This leaves clubs and spades which are touching in the sense that the two suits are next to each other. Indeed, the same rule should apply as it is much more economical to open 1♣ planning to rebid in spades than it would be to open 1♠ and rebid in clubs, especially as a response of, say, 2♦, would force opener to the three-level if he wanted to mention his clubs.

With 5-5 in two non-touching suits, open the major

With 5-5 in two non-touching suits, spades and diamonds or hearts and clubs, the answer is simply to open in the major suit.

For example, with:

♠	K3	(3 HCP)
♥	AJ765	(5 HCP + 1 DP)
♦	7	(0 HCP)
♣	KQ765	(5 HCP + 1 DP)

open 1♥. If partner responds 1♠, you have a very comfortable rebid of 2♣. However, if partner responds 2♦, the hand isn't really strong enough to push proceedings to the three-level so you should rebid 2♥.

three-suited hands

Without considering what you might do holding some totally bizarre distribution, all seems to fall into place. With a one-suited hand, say a six-card spade suit, you open 1♠ and rebid the suit. With a two-suited hand, open in your longest suit. With two 5 card suits, if you have two touching suits, open the higher suit, and, if you have two non-touching suits, open the major.

What about hands with three suits? If this means that you have a 5-4-4-0 distribution, the answer is to open the longest suit, however if you have a 4-4-4-1 distribution the answer is slightly more complicated.

Playing 5-card majors, your choice is restricted to opening either 1♣ or 1♦, the critical issue is to make sure that you have something to bid if partner responds in your singleton.

For example, with:

♠	7	(0 HCP)
♥	KQ65	(5 HCP)
♦	Q865	(2 HCP)
♣	AQ74	(6 HCP)

You could afford to open 1♣ rather than that moth-eaten diamond suit, as if partner responds 1♠ you can rebid 1NT.

However, make the hand a little stronger, say to:

♠	7	(0 HCP)
♥	AKJ5	(8 HCP)
♦	K865	(3 HCP)
♣	AQ74	(6 HCP)

Now, with 17 points you are too strong to rebid 1NT and not strong enough to jump to 2NT, and, unfortunately, you cannot open 1NT as this promises a balanced hand. So, if you open 1♣ and partner does respond 1♠, you will be totally stuck. This leaves you with little choice but to open 1♦, then if partner responds 1♠ you will have to

With 4-4-4-1 hands make sure you have a rebid if partner bids your singleton

make do with rebidding 2♣. Of course, it is not ideal, as partner will expect you to have five diamonds and four clubs and he certainly won't expect your hearts to be that good.

All this brings us to a really difficult hand. How should we cope with:

♠	AKJ5	(8 HCP)
♥	K865	(3 HCP)
♦	AQ74	(6 HCP)
♣	7	(0 HCP)

Systemically, it is clear that you should open 1♦. After all, the alternatives of 1♥ or 1♠ should promise a five card suit. However, if partner does respond 2♣, you have an almost impossible choice of evils. You can either rebid 2♥, pretending that you started with five diamonds or you can jump to 3NT pretending that you started with at least 19 points. Given, a choice of these two evils, I would elect to bid 2♥ in the hope that I will be able to bid 3NT on the next round.

responding

partner opens 1♣ or 1♦

weak hands

First of all, what is the minimum strength of hand that you should have before making a response to an opening bid of one of a minor?

Very simply, you know that for partner to open the bidding he must have a minimum of 13 points, but what is his maximum? He would open 2NT if he had a balanced 21 or 22 but he might just have as much as 19 or 20 points.

Respond with 6 points or more

As a total of 26 points is needed to have a reasonable chance of making game, it follows that if partner might have as much as 20 points then responder should find a bid with as little as 6 points. For example, holding:

♠ 75
♥ AQ643
♦ 864
♣ 864

you should respond 1 ♥ if partner opens either 1 ♣ or 1 ♦, but holding

    ♠ 975
    ♥ 106
    ♦ 963
    ♣ AJ752

you should pass if partner opens 1 ♦ but raise an opening bid of 1 ♣ to 2 ♣.

Yes, the hand has only five high card points but when partner opens 1 ♣, albeit guaranteeing only three clubs, you know that you have at least an eight-card fit so you can count one extra Support Point for the doubleton heart.

The top end of the weak range is a hand where you will no interest in game if partner has a minimum balanced hand. Opener's maximum is 15 points so with 11 points you would be interested in looking for game, hence the maximum for a weak hand is 9 or 10 points.

Now, suppose that your partner deals and opens 1 ♦ and the next hand passes, what should you respond on each of the following hands?

If you are going to raise partner, count your support points

(a)
- ♠ Q752
- ♥ 73
- ♦ 84
- ♣ KQJ75

(b)
- ♠ Q72
- ♥ 742
- ♦ K74
- ♣ QJ42

(c)
- ♠ Q72
- ♥ 72
- ♦ K742
- ♣ QJ42

answers

(a)   ♠ Q752
                    ♥ 73
                    ♦ 84
                    ♣ KQJ75

Holding hand (a) you have eight points, so clearly you have enough to respond, but which suit should you bid, spades or clubs? While you would always prefer to bid your longest suit first if you can, the problem with bidding your good club suit is that you would have to go to the two level to bid it, and you are not really strong enough to go that high, at least not without known fit.

The problem really is that your partner will continue to describe his hand. For example, if he holds a minimum balanced hand he might well rebid 2NT. Yes, of course, you would pass if he bids that, but 2NT is already likely to be too high. The alternative of bidding just 1♠ looks better because if partner does have a minimum balanced hand he will close the auction with his rebid of 1NT.

There is another significant advantage in bidding 1♠ rather than 2♣. In our system, partner would have to have five spades to open 1♠, so he could easily have a balanced hand with four diamonds and four spades and if we respond 2♣ we will miss our eight-card spade fit. If we respond 1♠ partner will be able to support us to 2♠.

In absolute terms, you should make every effort to find an eight-card major fit if you have one, so with this hand pattern you should always respond 1♠ to an opening bid of 1♦ unless you are strong enough to bid both of your suits. For example, if the auction starts:

1♦	Pass	2♣	Pass
2NT	Pass	?	

it should be fairly clear that if you bid 3♠ the auction is going to continue to the game level almost willy-nilly, so that you will need a hand strong enough to commit for game before you bid in this manner.

(b)

- ♠ Q72
- ♥ 742
- ♦ K74
- ♣ QJ42

A 1NT response shows at least 6 and no more than 9 or 10 points

Another eight point hand, but this time you don't have a major suit to bid nor do you have good diamond support, so what can you possibly bid? The answer is that you should respond 1NT, a limited bid showing about 6 to 9 or 10 points and denying a major suit or good diamond support.

(c)   ♠ Q72
                       ♥ 72
                       ♦ K742
                       ♣ QJ42

Holding hand (c) you also have eight high card points but in support of diamonds you can add on one support point taking the total to nine as you know that your side has at least 8 diamonds and you have a doubleton heart. Even with nine points the hand is still in the weak range so you should just raise 1♦ to 2♦.

intermediate or invitational strength hands

An intermediate strength responding hand is defined as one where there is some possibility of making game if partner has a minimum strength opener. For example, suppose your partner deals and opens 1♣ and the next hand passes, and you hold:

                     ♠ K75
                     ♥ QJ95
                     ♦ A75
                     ♣ J72

You have a decent four card heart suit so there is no problem on the first round, you respond 1♥, but then suppose that your partner's rebid is 1NT, which shows a balanced hand in the 13-15 point range.

Now you are in the genuine intermediate position, if partner is minimum you know that you do not have the values to sensibly try and make game but if he is maximum your combined hands will yield a total of 26 points and you should have good play for game. What can you do to get this message over?

The answer is that after partner rebids 1NT you should raise to 2NT. This is an invitational bid asking partner to pass if he is minimum and drive on to game if he is maximum for his rebid. Thus, intermediate strength hands fall into the range of 11-12 points

If partner rebids 1NT, raise to 2NT with 11 or 12 points

Now, what would you respond to an opening bid
of 1 ♦ on our next three examples:

(d)   ♠ Q752
                 ♥ 72
                 ♦ Q5
                 ♣ KQJ75

(e)   ♠ Q72
                 ♥ A42
                 ♦ Q74
                 ♣ QJ42

(f)   ♠ Q72
                 ♥ 75
                 ♦ KJ42
                 ♣ AJ42

answers

(d)   ♠ Q752

                 ♥ 72

                 ♦ Q5

                 ♣ KQJ75

As you can see, hand (d) is very similar to hand (a), having exactly the same shape but just a few more high cards to take it into the invitational range. (Notice that the 5 card club suit qualifies the hand for one distributional point.) Once again, the consideration comes down to which black suit should you respond in and once again 2♣ is flawed inasmuch as if partner rebids 2NT you really do not know what to do next? My guess is that the best shot would be to pass, but if opener has four spades you are likely to regret it.

So, with less than the values to force your partner to bid game, the right response is 1♠.

(e)   ♠ Q72

                 ♥ A42

                 ♦ Q74

                 ♣ QJ42

Surprise, surprise: this hand has the same shape as hand (b) but once again it is stronger having 11 points and therefore fits into the intermediate range. Too strong for a 1NT response you will have to make do with a response of 2♣. If partner rebids 2♦ you will have a convenient second bid of 2NT which once again shows a hand in the invitational range. However, if partner rebids 2NT himself then you face an awkward guess, if he is minimum you will be quite high enough but if he is maximum you might make game.

My own view would be that the right decision will be to pass a rebid of 2NT rather more often than not. The reasoning being that you have a very flat hand with no intermediate cards, no nines and tens and partner has a flat hand too otherwise he probably would have rebid 2♦.

Improve the hand to:

> ♠ QJ2
> ♥ A102
> ♦ Q74
> ♣ QJ92

and I would guess to bid 3NT over 2NT all the time. One more point and some potentially useful intermediate cards, the ♥10 and the ♣9.

(f)
          ♠ Q72
          ♥ 75
          ♦ KJ42
          ♣ AJ42

This hand is very similar to hand (c), once again it has the same shape but enough additional strength to make the hand fit into the invitational range. 11 HCP plus one support point takes the total to 12 and comfortably enough to invite partner to bid game. Give partner the good news and raise 1♦ to 3♦. This shows 4-card support and an invitational strength hand.

strong hands

> **A jump to three in partner's suit is invitational**

These are hands where you know that you should be in at least a game contract as soon as partner opens the bidding. By and large, if partner opens the bidding and you hold an opening bid yourself then you should definitely be in at least game, and, who knows, on a good day you might even be in the slam zone.

So, your partner opens 1♦, what would you respond on the following hands:

(g)
♠ KQ75
♥ 74
♦ Q5
♣ KQJ65

(h)
♠ Q72
♥ Q74
♦ AQ4
♣ QJ42

(i)
♠ Q72
♥ 74
♦ AQ42
♣ AJ42

(g)
♠ KQ75
♥ 74
♦ Q5
♣ KQJ65

This time you are strong enough to bid your suits in natural order. Start with 2♣ and if partner does rebid 2NT, that is fine, for you are plenty strong enough to continue describing your hand by bidding 3♠. If opener has four spades he will raise to 4♠, otherwise, he will either bid 3NT, preferably with a good holding in hearts, or support your clubs.

(h)

♠ Q72
♥ Q74
♦ AQ4
♣ QJ42

In response,
if you are
strong enough
for game, bid
your suits in
natural order

As in examples (b) and (e) you have a balanced hand, but this time with 13 points you already know that your combined strength with your partner should be enough to make game. Certainly, you might expect that 3NT would be the right contract but facing a hand like:

♠ 8
♥ AK52
♦ KJ987
♣ AK5

3NT would be very uncomfortable with the opponents probably being able to take five spade tricks while as you can see both 6♣ and 6♦ are virtually laydown. Just because you have a balanced hand doesn't mean that your partner has one too.

Clearly, it would be very convenient to have a bid that says that you have a balanced hand with game-going values leaving some space for exploring the alternative game-level contracts. Fortunately, in Standard American methods there

An immediate jump to 2NT facing a suit opening shows a balanced hand of 13-15 points

is just such a bid namely an immediate response of 2NT which shows a balanced hand in the region of 13-15 points.

If partner does have the strong 1-4-5-3 shaped hand shown above, he will undoubtedly begin to describe his shape by bidding 3♥, and the complete bidding sequence might be:

1♦	Pass	2NT	Pass
3♥	Pass	3NT(i)	Pass
4♣(ii)	Pass	4♦(iii)	Pass
6♦(iv)	All Pass		

(i) Difficult to think of anything else to bid at this stage.

(ii) Partner already knows that your combined assets put you in the slam zone provided that you do not have too much wasted in spades.

(iii) If you had very good spades the natural bid at this stage would be 4NT. You haven't got good spades and you do have quite good diamond support so it is time to show it.

(iv) Recognising that you would have bid 4NT rather than 4♦ with very good spades.

(i)

♠ Q72
♥ 74
♦ AQ42
♣ AJ42

This time you have four-card support for partner and a game-going hand, but it is far from clear whether 5♦ or 3NT will be best, and it is always possible that if partner has a good hand then a slam may be possible. So, how can you even start to get all this off your chest.

One possibility would be to start by responding 2♣ planning to support diamonds vigorously later but this would sounds like a much more shapely hand, a hand with five or six clubs and four diamonds springs to mind.

However, it seems clear that the specialised response of 2NT to show a balanced hand in the 13-15 point range is a much more descriptive choice. True, partner will not know that we have four card support for his suit. If he simply raises to 3NT you should call it a day but if he bids another suit then you will have the opportunity to show your good diamond support on the next round. For example, if he bids 3♥ as in the previous example it would seem appropriate now to jump to 5♦.

Finally, what should you bid if your partner opens
1 ♦ and you hold:

(j)   ♠ 75
                          ♥ AKQ1062
                          ♦ A5
                          ♣ K42

(k)   ♠ 75
                          ♥ AK1062
                          ♦ AQ105
                          ♣ K5

(l)   ♠ K74
                          ♥ AJ5
                          ♦ K43
                          ♣ AQ62

answers:

(j)
- ♠ 75
- ♥ AKQ1062
- ♦ A5
- ♣ K42

Rather like the opener, responder frequently needs to plan the campaign. If you start off just by making a simple 1 ♥ response and partner makes a minimum rebid such as 1NT or 2 ♦, you will have little option but to take a shot in the dark. Consider the following possible hands for opener:

(i)
- ♠ A642
- ♥ J73
- ♦ KQJ3
- ♣ Q7

(ii)
- ♠ KJ5
- ♥ 73
- ♦ KJ54
- ♣ AJ53

Both hands have a 4-4-3-2 shape with just 13 points but facing hand (i) you would make 12 tricks in comfort, the good diamonds providing discards for the losing spade after drawing trumps. However facing hand (ii) you would have to be very unlucky to go down in 4 ♥ but it is not beyond the realms of possibility. How then can we alert partner to the fact that there might be a slam on and enlist his help in determining just how high we should go.

> You can show slam potential by a jump response in a new suit

The answer is to make an immediate jump response of 2♥ on the first round, showing a hand not only strong enough to want to be in game but a hand that is likely to be interested in trying for slam. Having started off with a jump to 2♥, there will be no need to make a unilateral choice on the next round; if partner rebids either 2NT or 3♦ you can continue with just 3♥ which should convey the message that you jumped on the first round because you have a very good heart suit.

(k)
       ♠ 75
       ♥ AK1062
       ♦ AQ105
       ♣ K5

With 16 HCP in your own hand you know that you want to be in game as soon as partner opens the bidding, indeed playing in diamonds you can upgrade your hand to 18 points because you have two doubletons and you know that you have at least eight trumps between you. This puts you close to the slam zone even if partner has a minimum opener. Once again the time has come to get over your interest in exploring the slam zone by jumping to 2♥ on the first round but this time you will support diamonds on the next round. This will tell your partner why you were so enthusiastic when he opened 1♦

(I)

♠ K74
♥ AJ5
♦ K43
♣ AQ62

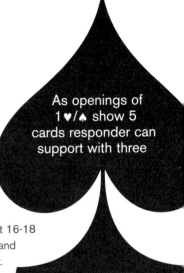

As openings of
1♥/♠ show 5
cards responder can
support with three

A balanced hand with 17 points, clearly enough for game and maybe enough for slam if partner has a medium strength hand. You are too strong for the immediate response of 2NT so bid 3NT showing a balanced hand with about 16-18 points without a good five card suit and without four card support for partner.

partner opens 1♥ or 1♠

There are two main differences between responding to one of a major compared with responding to one of a minor. They are:

1. Partner's opening bid shows a five card suit so frequently it will be possible to show partner that you have adequate support for his suit straightaway.

2. There is much less space to respond in a new suit at the one level so our choice of weak bids (or bids that may prove to be weak) is much more severely limited.

Let's go through the different strengths of hand once again.

You must
have at least
10 points to
respond in a
new suit at the
two-level

weak hands

With weak hands in the 6-9/10 point range, there are only three possible responses to an opening bid of 1 ♥. They are 1 ♠, 1NT and 2 ♥ and you would be even more restricted if partner opened 1 ♠. The choices then would be restricted to either 1NT or 2♠. As you need at least three trumps to support partner you are forced to bid 1NT with all sorts of hands without three or more cards in partner's suit. Your partner opens 1 ♥, what do you think you should respond with the following hands:

(a)
♠ Q752
♥ 75
♦ 64
♣ KQJ65

(b)
♠ Q72
♥ K742
♦ 75
♣ Q1042

(c)
♠ Q72
♥ 74
♦ K742
♣ QJ42

(d)
♠ Q75
♥ K74
♦ 96
♣ QJ965

answers:

(a)
♠ Q752
♥ 75
♦ 64
♣ KQJ65

If you are tempted to bid 2♣ don't! Of course, your club suit is the hand's best feature but a two level response must promise the values to go to at least 2NT as your partner might rebid that with a totally minimum hand. Your hand has only 8 HCP not the required 10 so bid 1♠ not 2♣.

(b)
♠ Q72
♥ K742
♦ 75
♣ Q1042

With four card support for your partner;s suit, obviously you are going to support him as you have already found a nine-card fit. However, even adding two points for the doubleton only takes your total to nine not enough to make an invitational jump to 3♥.

(c)
♠ Q72
♥ 74
♦ K742
♣ QJ42

This time you have no support for hearts and no four-card spade suit, but with eight points it is mandatory to keep the bidding open. So, what are you left with? Quite right, bid 1NT.

(d)
♠ Q75
♥ K74
♦ 96
♣ QJ965

Once again, if you are tempted to bid your long suit, don't. Your hand is in the minimum responding range, and apart from the fact that you are not strong enough to bid a new suit at the two level there is a much more important feature of your hand that partner needs to know. Your partner has at least five cards in hearts and you have three making a total of at least eight, so you already know that playing with hearts as trumps is likely to be best. Give your partner the good news straightaway by making a simple raise to 2♥. When your hand is only worth one bid, make the most descriptive one.

intermediate strength hands

Once again your partner opens 1♥, what would you bid on these slightly stronger hands?

(e)
♠ AQ75
♥ 64
♦ 75
♣ KJ1052

(f)
♠ A75
♥ K742
♦ 85
♣ K942

(g)
♠ Q72
♥ 74
♦ K104
♣ AQ753

(h)
♠ 75
♥ AJ4
♦ Q1054
♣ Q1076

answers

(e)
- ♠ AQ75
- ♥ 64
- ♦ 75
- ♣ KJ1052

This hand is just about strong enough to bid at the two level, however it is still better to respond 1♠. Why?

The answer is simply that if partner makes a minimum rebid such as 2♥ or 2NT you will be sorely tempted to pass yet you might then find that you have an eight-card spade fit. However if you respond 1♠, partner should raise you every time he has four cards in the suit and you have a fairly comfortable decision on the next round whatever he might choose to bid. If he rebids 1NT you could raise him to 2NT inviting him to go on to game with a maximum. If he rebids 2♣ obviously you will support him. If he rebids 2♦ it looks natural to continue with 2NT and if he just rebids his heart suit it looks sensible to pass. Once again, when choosing between alternatives it is a good principle to consider what you are going to bid on the next round.

Always consider what you are going to bid next time round

(f)
        ♠ A75
        ♥ K742
        ♦ 85
        ♣ Q1042

Yes, you only have 9 HCP but with four-card support for partner you can add two Support points for your doubleton diamond taking the total to 11 and well into the invitational range. With a combined total of at least 24 points you are only two points short of the magic total of 26 so jump to 3♥ inviting partner to press on to game if has anything more than a totally minimum opener.

(g)
        ♠ Q72
        ♥ 74
        ♦ K104
        ♣ AQ753

This time you have no real alternative to bidding 2♣ as you are too strong to respond just 1NT. If partner rebids 2♥ you have a comfortable rebid of 2NT, limiting your hand and inviting partner to press on to game with a good minimum opener but if partner rebids 2NT himself then you face an awkward guess. If he is minimum 2NT will be high enough; if he is maximum 3NT should be a make. With nothing else to guide you the most profitable decision in the long run is likely to be to press on to game, after all you score a big bonus if you make it.

(h)
- ♠ 75
- ♥ AJ4
- ♦ Q1054
- ♣ K976

10 HCP but if you support hearts you can add one for the spade doubleton. This takes you comfortably into the invitational range so bid 3♥, a limit bid inviting partner to press on to game if he has a bit more than a total minimum for his opening bid.

Don't forget to add in your support points

strong hands

Now lets look at some hands where when partner opens the bidding you already know that you have the values to play in game … or even higher ….

Your partner deals and opens 1 ♥, consider what you would respond on the following:

(i)
- ♠ AQ75
- ♥ J5
- ♦ 62
- ♣ KQJ65

(j)
- ♠ A72
- ♥ K742
- ♦ 75
- ♣ AJ65

(k)
- ♠ A72
- ♥ 74
- ♦ KJ74
- ♣ AQ42

(l)
- ♠ A73
- ♥ KJ74
- ♦ 7
- ♣ AQ543

answers:

(i)

♠ AQ75
♥ J5
♦ 62
♣ KQJ65

This hand has exactly the same shape as our previous examples (a) and (e); the difference is that, with 13 HCPs, this hand is much stronger so it is a reasonable plan to bid your suits in their natural order. So you respond 2♣. If partner rebids 2♦, your natural bid on the next round is 3NT. If partner bids 2♥ you have a comfortable continuation of 2♠, and if partner rebids 2NT you know you are going to game so you should have no qualms about bidding 3♠.

(j)

♠ A72
♥ K742
♦ 75
♣ AJ65

Like examples (b) and (f), once again you have four card support for your partner's major. With a known nine card fit, you can add two points for your doubleton diamond taking your total point count up to 14. You know that partner has at least 13, so give him the good news by raising his 1♥ opening to game. Bid 4♥.

(k)   ♠ A72
                       ♥ 74
                       ♦ KJ74
                       ♣ AQ42

A balanced hand, 14 HCP and no support for
partner. Give your partner the good news by
making an immediate jump response of 2NT
showing a balanced hand in the 13-15 point
range.

(l)   ♠ A73
                       ♥ KJ74
                       ♦ 7
                       ♣ AQ543

Now this is a pretty good hand anyway but when
partner opens 1♥ is becomes spectacularly good.
If you just count high card points you arrive at a
total of 14, you can add one for the five card club
suit anyway but when partner opens 1♥ you know
that you have nine trumps between you so you can
add three support points for the singleton
diamond, that all takes your total to 18 points and
with partner's minimum of 13 you already know
that you are close to the slam zone. For example,
at one extreme partner might have:

(i)   ♠ 85
                       ♥ AQ1082
                       ♦ A75
                       ♣ KJ4

when barring the most unlikely distribution you have a laydown grand slam available facing an opening bid which has no extreme distribution and only 14 HCP, but on the other hand, opener equally well might just have:

(ii)
- ♠ KQJ
- ♥ 108653
- ♦ KQJ7
- ♣ K

15 HCP facing your 18 should put you in the slam zone but apart from missing the ♦A you are also quite likely to lose two trump tricks meaning that anything higher than 4♥ could be dangerous.

So, how are we going to give partner the good news that we are interested in bidding a slam while giving ourselves some chance of stopping at a reasonable level if he has a totally unsuitable hand. The answer is to start by jumping to 3♣, showing a good club suit and some slam potential, and then support hearts on the next round to show that our enthusiasm was based on having a fit for partner.

For example, facing hand (ii) the whole auction is likely to be:

Opener	Responder
1 ♥	3 ♣
3NT(1)	4 ♥ (2)
Pass	

(1) With a minimum opener, no aces and very good holdings in the unbid suits, 3NT looks like the obvious rebid.

(2) If opener has most of his values in the pointed suits this will be high enough. No need to bid more as I showed my interest in slam with the jump to 3♣.

How you might bid a grand slam with confidence facing hand (i) is a much more complicated story and well beyond the scope of this book. However, if partner just raises your 3♣ response to 4♣ you should be confident of a massive fit in two suits and with the ace of spades and a singleton diamond covering the two unbid suits a simple jump to 6 ♥ would not be inappropriate.

partner opens 1NT

Responding to an opening bid of 1NT is totally different from responding to any other one level opening bid. As we have seen, most of the time it takes two bids to give a reasonable description of the opener's hand but a 1NT opening gets over the message in one go. Opener has between 16 and 18 points and a balanced hand so that you know that he has at least two cards in every suit. Before looking at what we might do with a range of weak, intermediate and strong hands, it is time to introduce you to your first conventional bid.

All over the world, bridge players use the bid of 2♣ in response to an opening of 1NT in a totally artificial manner, known as the Stayman Convention even though it was actually devised by Sam Stayman's partner of some 50 years ago, George Rapee. The 2♣ bid itself has nothing whatsoever to do with the responder's holding in clubs being used to ask the opener whether he holds a four card major. The basic scheme is quite straightforward. After a 1NT opening, responder bids 2♣ asking for four-card majors.

Opener responds:

2♦ with no-four card major
2♥ with four hearts
(with or without four spades)
2♠ with four spades
(but not four hearts)

This convention provides an easy route for responder to find out whether the partnership has a 4-4 fit in a major suit which is particularly helpful on game-going or game-invitational hands. The convention can also be used sensibly on some weak hands as we shall see.

weak hands

By definition, a weak hand facing a 1NT opener is one that has no interest in looking for game. A weak hand facing a one-level suit opening bid was defined as anything up to about 10 points, but here is you held 10 points and heard partner open 1NT showing 16-18 you would be confident of playing in a game contract. If partner has a maximum of 18 points then you need about 8 points to take you into the game invitational range, therefore a weak hand in this context is in the range of 0-7 points.

Now your partner opens 1NT, what would you bid holding:

(a)
♠ Q865
♥ K765
♦ 72
♣ 973

(b)
♠ Q8642
♥ K76
♦ 7
♣ 9763

(c)
♠ Q865
♥ K76
♦ J7543
♣ 7

(d)
♠ Q86
♥ 976
♦ 7
♣ Q109654

answers:

(a)   ♠   Q865
                     ♥   K765
                     ♦   72
                     ♣   973

Basically you have a balanced hand facing a balanced hand with a combined maximum point count of 23. You have no game ambitions and you have no reason to disagree with partner' suggestion that he plays in 1NT. Of course, holding four cards in both majors you might be tempted to try using your new Stayman toy. Undoubtedly, this will work well if partner happens to hold a four card major but if he doesn't a 2♦ response will leave you with nowhere to go. So, don't get involved just pass 1NT.

(b)   ♠   Q8642
                     ♥   K76
                     ♦   7
                     ♣   9763

With only 5 HCP again, you have no game ambition but your hand is much more likely to be of value playing with spades as trumps. Playing in no trumps even if your partner can establish your spade suit there is no guarantee that he will be able to return to your hand to cash them. However, playing with spades as trumps you are always likely to be able to make your long spades, either after clearing the opponents' trumps or by ruffing diamonds. Indeed, with a five card suit and a weak hand you should always remove the contract from 1NT into your suit at the two-level if you can. In this particular case, you should bid 2♠. Obviously this will not be possible with a five card club suit as 2♣ is Stayman, but with five of any other suit you should always take partner out of 1NT.

(c)
♠ Q865
♥ K76
♦ J7543
♣ 7

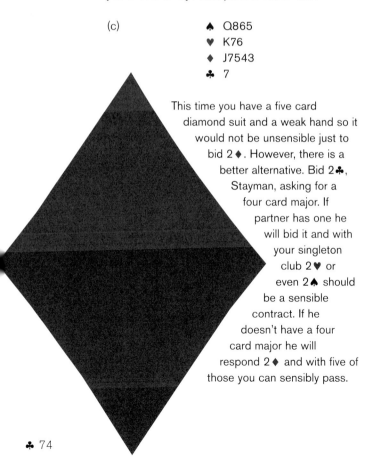

This time you have a five card diamond suit and a weak hand so it would not be unsensible just to bid 2♦. However, there is a better alternative. Bid 2♣, Stayman, asking for a four card major. If partner has one he will bid it and with your singleton club 2♥ or even 2♠ should be a sensible contract. If he doesn't have a four card major he will respond 2♦ and with five of those you can sensibly pass.

(d)

♠ Q86
♥ 976
♦ 7
♣ Q109654

While it is true that you would like to be able to bid 2♣ to play on this hand, adopting the Stayman convention means that this is impossible. However, all is not lost for you can bid 2♣ anyway and regardless of what partner responds you can follow up with 3♣ which is natural and to play.

So far, Stayman doesn't appear to be that useful but let's consider some stronger hands.

invitational hands

As before invitational hands are those that would like to be in game if opener has a maximum for his opening but would like to stop short if opener is minimum. Given that partner is in the 16-18 point range, this means that invitational hands will normally have 8 or 9 points. So, your partner opens 1NT what would you respond on the following hands:

(a)

♠ Q86
♥ K76
♦ J7543
♣ Q5

(b)
♠ K10864
♥ A76
♦ 7
♣ 9763

(c)
♠ Q865
♥ K103
♦ 72
♣ K765

(d)
♠ 986
♥ 97
♦ 76
♣ AQ10965

answers

(a)
♠ Q86
♥ K76
♦ J7543
♣ Q5

With 8 high card points and one distributional point
for the fifth diamond, this hand is full weight for an
invitational raise to 2NT, which invites opener to
pass with a minimum or bid 3NT with a maximum.

(b)
♠ K10864
♥ A76
♦ 7
♣ 9763

Only 7 HCP but full weight for an invitational bid showing five spades, as you can count one extra distributional point for the fifth spade. But how do we make an invitational bid to show five spades when an immediate bid of 2♠ is to play and not invitational. The answer is that you use Stayman first and then bid spades.

So you bid 2♣ and partner bids, 2♦ or 2♥, then you just bid 2♠. After all if you wanted to sign off in 2♠ you would have just bid it after the 1NT opening.

What would you do if partner actually responded 2♠ to your Stayman bid? Obviously you would support him but on this hand you should raise him all the way to game. Why? Well, now that you know that partner has four spades, you know that you have nine spades between you which means that you can add three points for your singleton diamond. What was 8 points has suddenly become 11.

(c)   ♠ Q865
                ♥ K103
                ♦ 72
                ♣ K765

At long last, a hand to use Stayman in straightforward fashion. You have four spades and enough to make an invitational raise to 2NT. So bid 2♣ - asking the opener if he has a four card major.

If he responds 2♦ or 2♥ just bid the 2NT that your hand was worth to start with. If he responds 2♠ just raise him to 3♠, once again inviting him to go on to game with a maximum.

(d)   ♠ 986
                       ♥ 97
                       ♦ 76
                       ♣ AQ10965

Only 6 HCP but our standard rule adds two distributional points taking the total to 8 and into the invitational range. However, on this occasion, our blanket valuation rule really does not do full justice to the potential power of this hand. Facing ♣Kx, the suit will provide 6 tricks most of the time making 3NT a very likely make facing a strong no trump. Indeed, even facing two small clubs there is a fair chance of making at least five tricks in the suit. On the down side, if the missing honours are both badly placed declarer might make no tricks in the suit, or maybe just one trick. One thing is for sure, depending how the club suit behaves we are either likely to make 3NT in comfort or fall a considerable number short, so trying to land on a knife-edge in an intermediate level contract such as 2NT is clearly pointless – either we make a lot of overtricks or we go down.

On balance, facing a strong no trump, this club suit is most likely to produce a lot of tricks so grasp the nettle and jump to 3NT.

strong hands

(a)
- ♠ AQ86
- ♥ K762
- ♦ J75
- ♣ 85

(b)
- ♠ KQ1086
- ♥ A76
- ♦ 73
- ♣ 976

(c)
- ♠ A86
- ♥ K103
- ♦ 72
- ♣ K7652

(d)
- ♠ AQ86
- ♥ J75
- ♦ K762
- ♣ 85

answers

(a)
- ♠ AQ86
- ♥ K762
- ♦ J75
- ♣ 85

With 10 HCP facing 16-18, you know that you have enough points for game, a minimum of 26.

So, it only remains to find the best game.
With two balanced hands, 3NT is the
obvious spot unless you have an eight-card
major suit fit. How are you going to find out?

Yes, this is an ideal hand for Stayman. You ask
opener if he has a four card major by responding
2♣. If he bids 2♦, denying a four card major, you
just bid 3NT, but if he responds either 2♥ or 2♠
you raise him to game in the major he has bid.

(b)   ♠ KQ1086
                            ♥ A76
                            ♦ 73
                            ♣ 976

Only 9 HCP this time but you can add one
distributional point for the five card spade suit,
taking the total to 10 and the combined minimum
point count to 26, enough for game. But which
game? It seems that you should play in 4♠ if
partner has three-card support or settle for 3NT if
he hasn't. How can you achieve this?
Very simply, jump to 3♠. This is forcing and offers
the opener a choice between 3NT and 4♠.

(c)   ♠ A86
                            ♥ K103
                            ♦ 72
                            ♣ K7652

This time you have a five card club suit and 10
HCP, so your total point count is 11 taking your

partnerships combined strength comfortably into the game zone. Just bid 3NT, of course it is possible that 5♣ will be better but only if partner has a very good fit for clubs and probably weak diamonds as well, but there is no sensible way of finding out.

(d) ♠ AQ86
     ♥ J75
     ♦ K762
     ♣ 85

Another balanced hand with enough values for game but this time the choice is between 3NT and 4♠ if partner happens to have four cards in that suit. So bid 2♣, Stayman. If opener bids 2♦ you just bid 3NT. If he bids 2♠, you have found a 4-4 fit so you bid 4♠. But what if he bids 2♥? Obviously you are not really interested in the fact that he holds four hearts, the problem is that he might also hold four spades. How do you find out?

In reality, the answer is that YOU don't. You just bid 3NT and he should know that as you would not have bothered using Stayman if you didn't have a four-card major, and as you have not supported hearts YOU must have four spades. If he has four spades as well he can convert 3NT to 4♠.

developing the auction

So, far we have concentrated on the principles involved in both the opener and responder describing their hands in the first two rounds of the bidding. Of course, sometimes when either the opener or the responder have given a good description of their hand quickly the bidding will not last very long but on many other occasions either player might need to find out further information or describe their own hand further before making a decision. Let's look at some examples:

Suppose that the bidding has started:

1 ♥	1 ♠
2 ♥	?

What would you bid next as responder holding the following hands:

(a)
- ♠ KJ763
- ♥ 104
- ♦ AJ9
- ♣ KQ4

(b)

♠ KJ763
♥ 5
♦ A854
♣ Q43

(c)

♠ KQJ63
♥ 104
♦ AK5
♣ 962

(d)

♠ AQ965
♥ A7
♦ 86
♣ J976

answers:

(a)

♠ KJ763
♥ 104
♦ AJ9
♣ KQ4

This hand is relatively straightforward. With 14 HCP of your own facing an opening bid, you know that you want to be in game and with excellent holdings in both unbid suits, the world and his dog would bid 3NT.

(b)

♠ KJ763
♥ 5
♦ A854
♣ Q43

This is harder, with cover in both unbid suits it is tempting to bid on with 2NT, however the right action is to pass. With absolutely no fit for your partner's suit be cautious. 2NT here invites partner to go on to game with a good hand for his bidding so far and your bad hear holding means that his main suit is likely to produce less tricks than he might expect.

(c)
- ♠ KQJ63
- ♥ 104
- ♦ AK5
- ♣ 962

This is more complicated than example (a). Once again, you have enough values for game but it is not clear what will be best 4♥, 3NT or even 4♠ and as you have no second suit, you are a bit stuck for a bid. So, what about trying 3♦, sure partner will think that you have a diamond suit but he is unlikely to support diamonds as if he had had four cards in the suit he might well have rebid 2♦ and not 2♥. After you have bid 3♦, you would expect your partner to bid 3NT on almost any hand with good clubs. If instead he bids 3♥, raise him to 4♥ and if he bids 3♠, press on to game in that suit.

(d)
- ♠ AQ965
- ♥ A7
- ♦ 86
- ♣ J976

This looks like a similar hand but it isn't. If you do bid 3♣, partner will bid on to game most of the time because he will expect you to have a better hand. Bidding a new suit at the three level shows a game going hand and this hand falls into the invitational range rather than the game-going range. So, how can you make a bid that shows that you still have an interest in making game but only if partner has got more than a total minimum.

One possibility would be to bid 2NT but your diamonds are particularly weak and nearly all your strength is in the majors. So, what alternative is there?

Why not make an invitational raise to 3♥? Think about partner's bidding. With only five hearts and a balanced minimum hand surely he should have rebid 1NT and if he had four cards in either clubs or diamonds he could have rebid in that suit. So, partner probably has six hearts. Is it not sensible to invite game in the major suit where you have an eight card fit.

Now, change chairs and suppose that you are the Opener after this sequence:

1♦	1♥
2NT	3♣
?	

What would you do next on the following hands:

(e)
- ♠ AJ10
- ♥ K5
- ♦ AKQ75
- ♣ J75

(f)
- ♠ Q76
- ♥ K5
- ♦ AKQ75
- ♣ AJ7

(g)
- ♠ Q76
- ♥ KQ5
- ♦ AKQ7
- ♣ J76

Answers

(e)
- ♠ AJ10
- ♥ K5
- ♦ AKQ75
- ♣ J75

First of all, what is partner trying to achieve? Well, yes, of course, he could have a very strong hand over there and just be describing his hand before making a slam try. However, that is pure speculation because he would also bid this way with a hand that just wanted to be in game but was uncertain as to the right strain. Certainly, in this situation, you should endeavour to show secondary support for partner's first suit but on this hand you only have two hearts. So what would you bid? Your holding in the unbid suit is so strong that 3NT seems the obvious bid.

(f)
- ♠ Q76
- ♥ K5
- ♦ AKQ75
- ♣ AJ7

This time you still have only two cards in hearts but your spade holding is relatively weak so 3NT doesn't look anywhere near so convincing. Is there an alternative?

Yes, partner doesn't know that you have five diamonds or that the suit is anywhere near this strong. So just bid 3♦ – in effect, this denies both three hearts and a good spade holding.

If partner continues with 3♥ you could raise to 4♥, and if partner bids 3NT you will figure that they should have some help in spades.

(g)
- ♠ Q76
- ♥ KQ5
- ♦ AKQ7
- ♣ J76

With three good hearts, the time has come to support your partner's suit. Bid 3♥

opening two clubs

Sometimes, you pick up such a strong hand that you would be scared to open at the one-level in case partner didn't have enough to respond and you might make a game (or even a slam). The solution in these cases is to open 2♣.

Rather like the Stayman convention, the 2♣ opening has nothing to do with clubs. It is a completely artificial bid just announcing that you have such a strong hand that your partner MUST keep the bidding open even if he has no points at all.

In just the same way as the 2♦ response to Stayman, the 2♦ response to a 2♣ opening is also a denial, but this time it denies a hand of about 7 points or more.

Any bid other than 2♦ in response to a 2♣ opening is a positive response, if responder bids 2NT opener should expect a balanced hand in the 7/8 HCP range, and if he bids a suit opener will expect a decent five card suit and at least a 'working' 7HCP.

So, consider how you would bid the following hands. If you choose to open 2♣, your partner will respond with a 2♦ negative, what would you then bid next?

(a)
♠ AK1076
♥ AKQ6
♦ KQ6
♣ 7

(b)
♠ AJ76
♥ AJ
♦ AQ865
♣ KQ

(c)
♠ AKQ9763
♥ AKQ4
♦ K6
♣ –

(d)
♠ A1097
♥ AKQ6
♦ KQ7
♣ AQ

answers:

(a)
      ♠ AK1076
      ♥ AKQ6
      ♦ KQ6
      ♣ 7

21HCP plus one distributional Point for the fifth spade only makes 22 and not really enough to guarantee making game unless partner has decent support for one of the majors. However, you should still open 2♣ as you would be a mite unhappy if you were left in 1♠ and found that you had a massive heart fit. If partner has a doubleton spade, and just four hearts headed by the jack you have some play for game. So, open 2♣, and over 2♦, bid 2♠. Responder must still keep the bidding open, so next time you can bid your hearts.

(b)
      ♠ AJ76
      ♥ AJ
      ♦ AQ865
      ♣ KQ

This is another 21 HCP hand with one distributional point taking the total to 22, however I would not consider opening this hand 2♣, preferring to open modestly with 1♦. There are two important differences between this hand and the previous example. The first hand had both majors and most of its high card strength concentrated in those suits. This hand has only one major and nearly half the strength in the outside suits. For example, facing a doubleton diamond and, say, ♠Qxxx you would need a lot of luck to make 4♠.

(c)
♠ AKQ9763
♥ AKQ4
♦ K6
♣ –

This is a real monster hand. Even if partner has no spades at all, you would not be too squeamish about playing this hand in 4♠. So, open 2♣, and, over the expected 2♦ response, jump to 3♠. Of course, you could just bid 2♠ and partner would have to bid again, so 3♠ is a specialised bid showing a very good suit of your own, and inviting partner to bid an ace if he has got one. As you can see, if partner bids 4♦ showing the ace of diamonds, a small slam in spades will be a decent contract. If partner bids 4♣ showing the ace of clubs, just settle for 4♠.

(d)
♠ A1097
♥ AKQ6
♦ KQ7
♣ AQ

24 points this time, so open 2♣ planning to rebid 2NT over the negative response. Once you have opened with 2♣ this is the only

sequence that the responder may pass, and even then you would expect him to bid on over 2NT with just 2 points.

Now, let's turn the tables and look at some responding hands. Partner opens 2♣, what do you respond holding:

(e)
♠ KQ754
♥ K4
♦ 752
♣ 983

(f)
♠ KJ754
♥ 84
♦ 752
♣ 983

(g)
♠ J8754
♥ K4
♦ K75
♣ 983

(h)
♠ 8754
♥ 973
♦ 752
♣ 983

answers:

(e)   ♠ KQ754
              ♥ K4
              ♦ 752
              ♣ 983

A classical positive response. Bid 2♠, you have a good spade suit and an outside working king.

(f)   ♠ KJ754
              ♥ 84
              ♦ 752
              ♣ 983

Facing a 2♣ opener, this hand isn't bad, but although you will want to mention your spades you are not strong enough to do so straightaway. Bid 2♦ negative, then bid your spades next.

(g)

♠ J8754
♥ K4
♦ K75
♣ 983

This time you have the values to make a positive response but your suit is quite poor. It is never a good idea to crowd the bidding when your partner has a good hand especially so when your bid might mislead partner. Best to bid 2 ♦, planning to bid spades next, and then later you can bid on to show your additional strength.

(h)

♠ 8754
♥ 973
♦ 752
♣ 983

A delightful hand. Tempting though it may be to pass partner's 2♣ opening, you must not. After all he is not even guaranteed to have any clubs. Respond 2 ♦, the artificial negative. If partner continues with 2NT you can pass for he will be showing a balanced hand with 23/24 points but if he makes any other bid you must carry on bidding until game is reached.

other opening bids

What about the other two-level openings. The reason why you will not find any details about other opening two bids here is that there is a multiplicity of ways in which you can play them.

Given the framework of our system, I would be inclined to choose to play the bids of 2♦, 2♥ and 2♠ to be natural and weak. Openings of this kind should show a decent 6-card suit and less than the strength to open the bidding – say, something like 7-10 HCP. Details of how to play Weak Two Bids will be found in another book in this series, How to Play Bridge: Simple Conventions.

The most obvious alternative to playing weak two bids is to play them as natural and strong. Indeed, in the early days most players would have treated an opening bid of 2♥ (say) as natural and forcing to game. However, an alternative school of thought grew up in England whereby an opening 2♥ was natural and showed a hand not quite strong enough to force to game. In this method an opening bid of 2♥ bid could not

be passed but the auction could stop in
3 ♥ if the responder had nothing.
More recently, two level openings have
been used to show all types of hand,
ranging from real opening bids frequently
of a two-suited or three-suited nature down
to very weak hands where all the opening
bidder is trying to achieve is disruption of his
opponent's bidding. The list is endless and
getting bogged down in these ideas is way
beyond the scope of this book.

Opening bids at the three and four level are weak
but based on a long suit so that if your opponents
should choose to double, the penalty will not be
that severe. Because such opening bids make life
a lot more difficult for the opponents they are
known as pre-emptive openings.

Vulnerable, a 3♠ opening might show:

        ♠ KQJ9654
        ♥ 6
        ♦ J86
        ♣ 86

whereas non-vulnerable it might be a bit weaker say:

        ♠ AJ98652
        ♥ 6
        ♦ J86
        ♣ 86